What Love Requires

Dana Littlepage Smith

Oversteps Books

First published in 2020 by   Oversteps Books Ltd
                                6 Halwell House
                                South Pool
                                Nr Kingsbridge
                                Devon
                                TQ7 2RX
                                UK

www.overstepsbooks.com

Copyright © 2020 Dana Littlepage Smith
ISBN 978-1-906856-88-5

All rights reserved. No part of this book may be reproduced, stored in a retrieval system, or transmitted in any form, or by any means, electronic, mechanical, photocopying, recording or otherwise, or translated into any language, without prior written permission from Oversteps Books, except by a reviewer who may quote brief passages in a review.

The right of Dana Littlepage Smith to be identified as the author of this work has been asserted by her in accordance with the Copyright, Designs and Patents Act 1988.

Printed in Great Britain by imprint digital, Devon

*This book is for Cynthia Gill and for Quaker friends
and for all who stand in the great cloud of witnesses.*

*Attend to what love requires of you,
which may not be great busyness.*

From Advices & queries 28. Quaker faith and practice, © 2013
The Yearly Meeting of the Religious Society of Friends in Britain.

Acknowledgements

Some of these poems were written during a Hawthornden Fellowship for which I am grateful.
Domestic was published in Image: A Journal of Faith and Mystery.
Edited versions of *Poems for Megan Boyd* and *To a Man Given a Lake for his Retirement* were published in Stand.
A version of *Bishop Winchester's Geese* was published by Myslexia.
Words for Doris Pigeon, The Children in Quaker Meeting, Looking for Cows, A Quaker Woman Sends a Christmas Card to Donald, The Sibyls Speak in Quaker Meeting, Why I Wear your Socks Today and *Anxiety* were published by The Friend.

A variety of these poems appeared on a CD, with music composed by Stephen Tanner.

I am grateful to Christine Considine and Charles Montgomery who kindly read and responded to drafts of this manuscript.

Contents

My Father Considers	1
Sitting with J in The Clouds of Unknowing	2
A Quaker Woman Sends a Christmas Card to Donald	3
Words for Doris Pigeon, Quaker	4
For A Man Speaking in Quaker Meeting	5
The Children in Quaker Meeting	6
Anxiety	7
Looking for Cows	8
The Sibyls Speak in Quaker Meeting	9
Penelope's Preserves	10
A Lover Once Left	11
The Haircut	12
When Lightning Struck our Mare	13
Feathers and Phantoms	14
On the Dee, Spey, Lochy	15
Kissing the Water	16
Sundays, She Disappeared	17
To a Man Given a Lake for his Retirement	18
To a Child Learning the Clock's Face	19
For Vladimir	20
Michelangelo's Snowman	21
Meriwether Remembers	22
Bishop Winchester's Geese	24
Lies	25
Wolf Sister	26
Flames	27
As Military Jets Fly Low over the Fields of Devon	28
Absence	29
Inhabit Me	30
Portrait	31
The Fat Birds of Capitalism	32
Domestic	33
Carolling With Pinhoe Road Baptist Church	34
Plum Lovely	35
Simeon's Song: First Communion	36
In Jerusalem Dust Speaks	37
The Children of Port-au-Prince	38

To a Boy Making a Paper Hat	39
Nothing Lives in One Dimension	40
Year Seven Visits The Wanderer	41
For Sandra, Who Drew a Tree	42
Overheard: Ringing in the Changes	43
Why I Wear your Socks Today	44
Understory	45
Life on Mars	46
Brent Geese Among Eelgrass	47
Black Fire	48
Will Kemp Goes Dancing	49

My Father Considers

When in the course of human events it becomes hard
to stand as my father finds, aged eighty-nine,
leaning against the kitchen sink, he begins to speak
of the men who collect our garbage. *Endowed by their Creator
with certain unalienable rights ... among these: Life, liberty
and the pursuit of happiness.* My father's creed
is located in the trials, the laughter of these men
who are central to our happiness. While the fat cats,
with their machinations and mean-spirited greed
believe inequality necessary *as humans are disposed to suffer,
while evils are sufferable.* As when in the course of cold
November and its rain, these men help my father carry
his weight of waste and recyclables up to their truck.
With each step, they are mindful of his decomposing spine,
his right foot with no feeling which might as well be
trawling the surface of Mars. My father understands
their separate yet equal station; these men who work
uninsured, without health care or pensions
through the night until they arrive here at his doorstep,
willing to help him surmount the last difficult steps
of black ice back to his waiting plate of strawberries,
warmth and coffee. These men who bear our history,
its failures and its momentary glories on their backs,
help him, an elder on his way, amidst the storm strew
of yesterday's news, not knowing if he is one with them,
or one of the others *who harass our people, and eat out
their substance.* He jokes with them about the slog
of growing old: that downhill slide which is all uphill work.
They smile. These men who understand grief's strong hands:
my father says *are among the powers of the earth,* riding on
the tide of dawn, on and on into our night, collecting garbage.
*Having been endowed by their Creator with certain
unalienable rights, that among these are the pursuit of
happiness. Liberty and life.*

The lines in italics are taken from The Declaration of Independence.

Sitting with J in The Clouds of Unknowing

I lie on the floor at her feet,
in a wide slice of sun with the cat,
her sweetheart, who sleeps alongside
her in her husband's bed.
I lie on the floor and say little
while the boat of her small cedar
house rolls through the clouds.
Her rooms spread wide a pool
beneath the blue spruce
with only the listening wind
and the billowing curtains
for sails as we read the occasional
line from the *Cloud of Unknowing*.
But mostly we do nothing
as J springs to her feet
or kneels on the floor, lithe at ninety-
five, luring her fat sweetheart cat
close beside us. The world pours in
very lightly. Green fields hold our city,
ripeness swells. *Owning nothing—*
J recalls the monks who first
found her — *yet possessing all things.*
Love too is not to be got by thought
she reminds me, as we close our eyes
waiting, simply waiting, whether or not
it arrives in the big sea-green sky
of Monterey pines: *God's syllables*
which contain nothing we can think.

The Cloud of Unknowing *was written anonymously in the late 14th century.*
It is considered one of the great works of Christian medieval mysticism.

A Quaker Woman Sends a Christmas Card to Donald

This woman burns a mouse-bitten pinch
of wax that passes for a candle, as she focuses
the diamond of her mind on Donald.

She breathes in her Welsh hills, savouring
the milk-green of reindeer lichen,
the glisten on each jar of beets.

The cherishing of small things is her way
of combating hate and greed.
She marvels as a spider extends

its silken self more fluidly than steel
spanning the centuries of our inattention.
As a sparrow feeds itself

into a piece of scaffolding, she watches
as it tests the darkness. Once, twice,
then backs out to re-interpret sky.

She polishes her window panes
with apple cider vinegar,
welcoming the fire

in the rose-hips. It's then
she notices a tear of blue,
a deeper field reclaiming sky.

Words for Doris Pigeon, Quaker

I've no idea Doris, what love
required of you. Though your name
this morning was mentioned in meeting.
Like a light, blown skyward.
The ash of a woman on her way.

Dorothy Partridge, they might
have said, or Betty Peacock.
But they didn't. It was Doris
Pigeon. A name I sit with in my shed.
Sunday night, dusk grown fig-deep
yet somehow in that dark, a light.

Love never needs a sense of self-
accomplishment. Doris Pigeon,
in her end may have only
sat watching witless birds dawdle,
sun baubles, rainbowed
on a lawn of darkening light.

For A Man Speaking in Quaker Meeting

Blitzed by all the ordinary
uncertainties, he paused.
At first he heard chaos
at the stoplight.
Was flooded by
an orchestra of losses.
Seeing a friend, incontinent,
every orifice chancy
reminded him of a widow
smearing a smile
on her loneliness
each evening.

Then came the quiet
of something lyrical
like an old acquaintance.
Acceptance belled
in a big wind like
a sheet in summer.
Hardships, heavy,
continued to fall
among the bits
of remembered gladness.

The Children in Quaker Meeting

The children in Quaker Meeting
are learning about different sorts
of insulation: newspapers
on the ground work for rough sleepers.
Bubble-wrap pillows will lie on asphalt.
For the lucky, there's ewe's wool in the attic,
layer upon layer of lanolin blessing.

The children in Quaker meeting
are baking cookies to teach us
the ways of the world: to make us
feel the weight of *the haves* and
the have nots. They tell us there will not
be enough for us all so if we get a biscuit,
be grateful and remember
how it felt when the smell of still hot
chocolate and macadamia nuts
swelled the room of our senses.

Anxiety

I asked anxiety to dig one hole.
It worked until the green sward
of our garden was gauged into a mole field.

Anxiety needed to be busy,
it filleted the lawn like the herring gull;
incessantly flapping.

It cawed. I focused
on the sparrows,
easy in the wind-flowers.

Finally, I decided
to do nothing. For days
and days, until the night

the moon gave enough
light for me to fill
a seed-bed.

Maybe when we can breathe
with one another again,
I'll invite our neighbours

to sit beneath Mexican
sunflowers. Their gold heads
looming late into fall.

And if nothing
blooms that too
will have to serve:

contemplating the places
where something small
was planted and tended for a season.

Looking for Cows
after Meister Eckhart

We went looking for God
the way one looks for a cow,
expecting warm flanks, soft cheese.
All the universe ran away
from us, its rivers of milk
lit a way for us
but we were too busy
looking for cows
in dark byres.
We kept our eyes
down, burrowed
toward cowpats
while all the world
stayed awake for us —
but we were looking
for meat we could skewer
in our little fires.
The spheres of delight
were already disappearing,
singing in flames
for us. But we were busy,
we had something better
to do — looking for cows.

The Sibyls Speak in Quaker Meeting

The last bird sang
its black remembrance

of earth at the bottom
of our garden, one blackbird

perched on the edge of time
like a spindly twig, May-

quickened. Its golden beak
needled its way into the sheer

nothingness of the last day.
It sang, *I am all of what is ...*

A black remembrance.
I am the bison's shadow.

I am the mourning
in the dove's song.

I am the bowed head
of Himalayan poppy.

I am the Golgotha
of Beluga whales,

the skull of hills
still gleaming. I am

a ninety year-old woman
witnessing to what I have seen,

shaking like an aspen tree
in Quaker meeting.

Penelope's Preserves

The last words her husband spoke to me,
Are those apples on your tree for picking?
'Yes, come round sometime,' I smiled.
Weeks after he died, I met his wife at the threshold
of our door, beneath the flames that flared
across the sky. She was gathering the last
of the fruit, some of it bruised, late in the season.
She made them into a preserve, placed a jar
in my hands as I was leaving Quaker Meeting.
I do not know if apples, honey, cinnamon
and raisins constitute prayer, yet they contain
silences, the wooded acres between
her thoughts, her heart full as she chopped apples.
No darkness is entirely desolate. The light
that played in her husband's eyes when he asked
about our old tree, he passed on to me.
I taste the happiness of apples he was glad to see.
We live in the bright shadows of such consolations.

A Lover Once Left

A lover once left
a yellow sheet
of lined paper
on my desk.
On it he had drawn
a treasure chest,
a jewel bed
darkly sparkling.
Beneath it
he had written:
*It's always here
for the taking ...*
He walked his ways,
his depths of emerald
hills, his sapphire nights.
*Love to your most
unloved places.*

The Haircut

He did not mention his tracheotomy, the hole
the size of a nickel, nicked in his throat.
Did not say a dark *O* travelled with him each day.

He told me to look for a man with a cane.
He brought pygmy songs and Gregorian chants.
Took up scissors, used his fingers for a comb.

The afternoon fell silent. My hair was rinsed
by a stranger, high in the eyrie of my loft
above the city. We spoke little;

each took what was offered.
I remember the light as it fell.
And I found myself on Zakynthos

with a lizard, each of us drinking
a world from a pearl
of water.

When Lightning Struck our Mare

When lightning struck our mare,
she leapt then folded to the ground
like a swan for whom death is
a friendly river.

When lightning struck our mare,
my mother laughed in fear. A hive
swarmed from her mouth, my lover
whispered a shovel as if hard ground

would heave its sods and help her
dig an opening to a new language.
Our mare bolted, her colt stuttered
through a dream of a thousand

seedheads, spores lifted the field
like a psalm too sacred to be lost.
Yet we had mislaid it, that shining song,
our birthright, the *shibboleth* of summer.

Feathers and Phantoms

Megan Boyd of Brora in Sutherland was hailed by many as the finest fly-tier in the world.

For fifty years she lived within the wilderness
of fourteen hour days. So when
the Queen invited her to London
she couldn't go. It was bingo night in the local.

She wilded in her shed until the world came
to find her. Expert at the flies: for the tag
she used a twist of cream and crimson silk.
Phantom hands filched the fantastic from thin air.

Always beneath the ice, the flow.
A single deft-eyed salmon homing.
Two turns of blue seal fur for the body.
Head down, she kept the seasons close:

sweet peaseweep, the blirty and the blinter.

On the Dee, Spey, Lochy

When Miss Boyd asked to cut my hair,
I was sixteen. I flamed.
Later over strong tea,
she took a sprig of claret mohair
from my jumper.
She snipped one strip of cream
coloured turkey. Long hours
we spent lost in reveries
of feathers: cock-hackle of long-fibber.

It is lifetimes since I sipped tea
at her kidney-shaped table ...
Yet the touch she might have taken
still wakes me in my dreams.

Kissing the Water

She knew it was life and only life
that caused the fish to bite,

the fly must kiss the water.
To fish would mean to kill

the fish. So she didn't.
Ever.

She auctioned her flies to buy the nets
which blocked the few returning salmon.

The stocks of baby sand eels
like a *smirr* of rain were disappearing.

She watched from her kitchen window
as trawlers scooped them up.

The feast now turned to starving.
Her buried memory of salmon smolts:

a skirl of pipes dissolving.

Sundays, She Disappeared

There were sightings:
some toff would say he'd seen her,

buck-naked in the Blackwater,
the Beaully. A stalker would claim

to have spotted a patch of red
pig's wool, an Eton crop trotting

through fir forest. A snatch
of something other. A fire-flash.

A whisper of jay's cackle.
It certainly wasn't church

she sought. Had little
to do with other people.

She seamed her way, canny.
A lone woman, knowing not

to break surface. Just braid
her way into dark muscle.

Become the living water.

To a Man Given a Lake for his Retirement

He tells them to skip the whip round
for the watch. Plash and mizzle

is all he wants. Whitehall
far behind him.

The world is lit with possibility:
this dark lake ...

How long was he dead
to hawkmoth, chickweed?

The errata of his days
takes flight.

Now the solitary wasp
is his companion.

A pint and an afternoon
with the gooseberry sawfly

makes him reel with
meadowsweet and pupae.

To a Child Learning the Clock's Face

We are left pretending that
numbers marching round
a circle can teach us
time, that cartwheel
of a life. You are tired,
so say, *It is 7 past 16.*
Right. Time
to a six year old
is a wood of moorland
yellows. The pearl-edged
fritillary sweeps its wings
across our faces,
a second and a second
flies. Then a life.
To say that this
antenna of an arrow
can keep the course of time
is, of course, a lie.
The tortoiseshell sips
a moment's nectar;
the sun is swallowed
by a grizzled skipper.

For Vladimir

He is Russian so does not apologise
for speaking to the birch like a sister.
Here we need only two chairs.
The leaves are our music.
Not Stravinsky. Humbler, sweeter.

Vladimir insists I listen to the difference
between the oak and the chestnut.

He turns the taps
in the cemetery to make puddles
beneath brambles
for squirrels and foxes
before he disappears, a priest
into his vespers of long shadows.

Michelangelo's Snowman

One winter, when a great deal of snow fell in Florence, Piero de' Medici had Michelangelo make, in his courtyard, a statue of snow, which was very beautiful.

                      Vasari

My hands were blued
with cold so I modelled
quickly. I made a beauty
out of ice. Snow balls
I lit with embers of fire
to make his sex glow.
I was happy, hungry,
a lad not yet twenty.
Curs cocked their legs
adding a pair of golden
slippers to my David.

Beggars and urchins circled.
I stayed awhile among
the motley of those who
happened by: cripples
and thieves who know
all things give light.
We moved on memory's
black ice. While his snow
flesh of topaz melted,
all turned to slush
beneath the sun's old eye.

Meriwether Remembers
She was so strong. So hard to die

I thought Charbonneau
had won the sky
when he was given her.
She was Sacagawea,
Shoshone, a maiden.
She walked the rivers
of three languages.
She dug wild liquorice.
Her weight was warmer
than gold, sweeter
than prairie apples.
When we needed to eat,
she traded her belt of turquoise.
In the gamble for Montana,
she surprised the mice
by digging their winter hoard.
She took only what was
needed: five artichokes
not long buried.
Pilot to the Yellowstone
and every river, she became
my hills, my valleys.

And yet she died alone.
The iron tongues of Fort
Manuel, in my mind,
are still clanging. She
was just twenty-five,
sleeker than a sea otter.

Now she lies seventy miles
from Bismarck.
The cold has blued
her toes like corn.
She, the one woman
for whom I should have
upended Bitterroot and
every other mountain.

Toussaint Charbonneau (1767-1843) was a French-Canadian trader who purchased or won Sacagawea, a Shoshone girl from the Hidatsa, a native American people. In November 1804, Meriwether Lewis and Clark, explorers of the American west, came to the area, recruiting Charbonneau as a translator. They were more eager to have the Shoshone women join them.

Bishop Winchester's Geese

My girls, my geese, I keep them a stone's throw
from the Thames, in Southwark's sweet shadow.

Unconsecrated? No. I blessed them, each.
Lucy was pure as a choirboy's *Agnus Dei*.

Her poor tricks were given for a penny,
until her eyes flared and her sores flamed.

Mad Maude has lived to a ripe age.
Her whore-son rhymes make Bedlam's men blush.

Christ's bones but she did keep the angel-maker
in good trade. Nights when I cannot sleep,

I go down to see her. She's poxed, near blind.
Yet wise enough to laugh at me. To her,

my garnet gown and festering gold
mean nothing. My sin is simple:

I believed that power was mine
so I was used by power. Now Maude spits

and greases her woman's mark o'er me.
No cross, just an ever-widening circle.

A chicken-legged old man, I'm pot-bellied, limp.
The love of my old geese could letter me

into true learning if I could submit to them,
my girls, too thin to survive this winter.

---

*In 1161, Henry of Blois, Bishop of Winchester earned a wage from
prostitutes in Southwark, London. They were called his 'geese' and were
buried in unconsecrated ground near Southwark Cathedral.
Angel-maker, a euphemism for abortionist, comes from Penelope
Fitzgerald's book,* The Blue Flower.

Lies

Falsehood flies, and Truth comes limping after it.
                                    Jonathan Swift

The lies came easily
at the end, as easily
as fire counterfeiting light
until it swallowed
darkness. As easily
as darkness sexing
a starless sky into night.
O there were noble lies
which fell like Plato's rain
engendering the social
harmony: dissimulators
until the end of time.
But no one knew
where the roots,
the steadfast ones,
had burrowed
in our post-truth world.
Light seemed to slip away,
some said it still illumined ...
All the while, the lies
came fast as funerals
for glaciers. Meltwater
brimmed our eyes.
Truth and beauty
might have blinked
as falsehood
danced its thin red line
over the horizon.
The suicides
became fake news.
False witness
worked overtime.
Our blinded eyes
reminded us of something.

Wolf Sister
A Latvian Woman Sells the President a Pair of Socks

They waited in forest lairs for seventeen winters:
through the joke of Latvia and her liberators.
First Soviet, then Nazi ...

As they gathered summer's meadows
for pots of tea to share among neighbours,
she held the yarn of politics, her gnarled hands

fingering each inch of its story.
When the president paid for a pair
of cloudberry socks, she would not smile

for the camera. She knew he would
never wear them as she prayed
her children would never taste

his coca cola. Or worship his dollars
which cannot comprehend
the height, the depth of earth's altar:

its forests of dew and blue gentian.

Flames

Refugees reach new limits: they burn
their fingerprints until they won't grow back.
Their paperwork drowns in a sea of sorrow.
No one can say what brings the chance of a visa.

Once it was decreed: *they shall die
grievous deaths. They shall not be
lamented, neither shall they
be buried.* Only then did we see

our faces grown strange,
our losses bled into theirs.
We saw our eyes brim, tears slip
as we looked out from this day's pages.

As we watched, another thousand
thousand species slid into white space.
All the while, the margins of our lives,
unseen worlds, grew thinner.

Quotation from Jeremiah 16, verse 4

As Military Jets Fly Low over the Fields of Devon

Fury shakes the sky
while the lone bull bellows.

Dogs splay themselves flat
as rugs in Victorian shadows.

The chickens' stutters stop.
We all freeze, mid-stride.

Shock breaks in waves.
Sheep scatter in the simple dread

of humans who rarely breathe a word
of death, yet worship it like a father.

Absence
for the students of Marjory Stoneman Douglas High School

I lug frozen pails of snow to melt inside.
Absence lives in the meltwater of time,
endured because it must be endured
like blizzards or a shattering light.
Radiant absence blinds as it beckons
a walk in snow so bright I stagger.
Absence binds us, one to another.
Absence says, I will not rest.
I will live in bullets and in breasts.
I will feast on the everyday air.
Yes, we have the right to be afraid,
terrified when a desk topples
with a pop! or a car backfires.
Mom — the text reads, and then
stops ... *Absence, my friend,*
where will you go? And when?

Inhabit Me

Inhabit me ants, wasps, blue whales.
Inhabit me sense of scale
which translates us into
minuscule dominions.

Inhabit me screech
owl signalling the dark;
bats of the cranny, peppered moth
wing me into non-human frontiers.

Inhabit me live oak, dead
elm branching into primordial air.
Gospel chorus of trees sing
your earth-girdle of green around me.

Amazon emblazon your loss
in my marrow. Tattoo me
with your great fires. Inhabit
me wastes of the earth.

Wake me into your creative desolation.

Portrait

I asked if I could make her portrait with charcoal,
red dust, black dung dug from our garden.

I wanted to sketch her more
than survival, her ripping laughter,

that spilled out like well-water.
Her wounds weren't my interest.

Her breath-by-breath was. She gave it
simply, like sphagnum moss

brought to the Somme from Dartmoor.
In war, green Devon came to staunch

the blood of the near-slaughtered.
Nature's antiseptic: moss from the bog.

I drew the loose lines of her witness,
her inward defiance, venturing on.

The Fat Birds of Capitalism

Today the fat birds of capitalism
have flown into a great wind,
while the seeds of charity
are scattered richly
in poor neighbourhoods
where bread arrives
in floury paper; neighbours
baking through the night.

With news of the virus,
the gated communities remain
locked and gated. Insider trading
panics: *Dump your stocks,*
this thing will be bigger
than anything that can unite us ...

Except, I see from my front window,
the fear-mongers might be wrong:
a child runs into the onslaught
of our cemetery with fistfuls of sun,
dandelions scattered prodigally
at the feet of each passerby.
She makes a dance of social distancing,
a side-step and a spring, leaping
over that which was scrawled
on last night's pavements:
rainbows bleeding new worlds
magenta, poppy, green beneath our feet.

Domestic

The world hung heavy
on her breast.

Someone snipped
an umbilicus,

she homed him:
Love's foundling.

Beneath the shower of comets
the shepherds lit dried dung.

Kings came and slunk away.
Night clambered on

atop another day. Close
by a spark or two

of life's Unknown
caught flame:

his light, storm-fast
falling to wyrd fire.

The word wyrd *is Old English meaning fate, chance or fortune.*

Carolling With Pinhoe Road Baptist Church

Bum parked by the radiator,
I thought it better to drink
scotch neat and eat salmon.

My husband wouldn't have it.
*The street lights will make pools
enough to read by.*

We stepped into the star-jumps
of excited kids, while others
skipped to keep their blood fast

pumping beneath the sky-bright
glister. The woman beside me
wore a wool cap, was small

yet laughed at the cold.
Her pension ran
to an old stone house,

kitchen and bedroom half-heated.
When she opened her mouth,
she took her own route.

She wove around our big braid
of song: her counterpoint
was a skinful of music.

Her notes fell on dark houses:
pinpoints of shining. Her voice bid
wild kids jump through *Jingle Bells*.

Listeners ventured out
from flats, wrapped in blankets.
One or two were already in pyjamas.

A widow and her dog
were crowned by stars,
their heads leaned so far out of the window.

Plum Lovely

My gran said, Jesus came
to Abergavenny
just the once, plum lovely.

He knew the thin places
where the wind
blows the heart

to slate grey stone:
Crinow, Cold Blow,
Conway. She claimed

he was an alien
who walked
the Pendine Sands

with a stale bun
and a roll up.
Will you be with us?

Gran had the sense to ask.
He stayed. We thawed,
ate fish with him.

Our voices sang us
into this weave of words
I keep wrapped around me.

Simeon's Song: First Communion

For a boy of nine, the bible is not so deep
as the electron collider

where he would like to sleep.
Nothing is something you know,

he confides in me. His smile is wildly shy.
God is the nothing he feels

most brightly at night. He knows
no lines can confine Him.

This first communion book is a riddle.
Why should he care about the colour of Jesus?

He chops his own hair with gluey scissors,
tapes his fine threads on Our Lord's head.

He grins at the mousey halo he has made
for his friend without nest or den.

In Jerusalem Dust Speaks

What is good? the children ask.
Our school is field and rubble.

Dead meat blooms in our well.
Salt harrows our orchard.

In *The Daily News,*
dust gets scant measure.

In video-replay,
it lacks the substance of shadow.

Children sing the sun
down, scavenging in rubbish.

Mercy waits in the hosepipe
which might fill tonight.

Black lemons rot.
Olives ruin into yellow.

The Children of Port-au-Prince

I drank the hot milk of Haiti,
as I watched forty children
run up a hill from the shanty town
of corrugated sheds
where they rented sleep:

six hours of it in daylight.
Rest was cheaper from dawn
to noon so they nailed black plastic
to windows and prayed for dreams.

I drank milk when they had none.
Guilt curdled me. When curfew fell,
Henri waited on the roof outside
my room like a mother waits
in the dark, the whites of his eyes shining.

The children slipped drawings
under my door, snakes
twisted into Christ's cross,
a rainbow-coloured redemption
alive with mango and frangipani trees.

Even the youngest in the orphanage,
bread-thief, survivor, left notes:
*I pray for you. You good
my friend for me.* Forty years
later and still they come.

Dancing, drumming, laughing
in my sleep, they pull me
into the dance, asking,
*Are you ready yet
to be befriended?*

To a Boy Making a Paper Hat

He cuts a halo from today's news.
His word-nest becomes a world
grown by buttresses of paper.

When I say he can bin the scraps,
he laughs and weaves the trash
into a garland.

Mum arrives and he leaves it
all behind: his cap
with its brimful of stories

of climate wars, wells drying.
A mizzling sleet descends.
I stand in front of our cathedral

wearing his hat
lit by stars long dead,
the darkness not yet overcoming.

Nothing Lives in One Dimension

My neighbour arrives
strange as a baroque
angel. He tickles me

with a feathered stick
and tells me nothing lives
in one dimension.

He follows me like a stray
cat down our hall,
poking at the fabric

of our lives,
enlarging my idea
of the day ...

He sticks his green tongue
into my controlled space.
Nothing lives in one dimension,

he reminds me,
the gobstopper on his tongue
another imploding planet.

Year Seven Visits The Wanderer

When time's crow-footed passage
sped us on from English class
into the Bishop's Palace,
we snubbed our noses to the glass.
We steamed the cube of that room,
like magpies come to steal
life's hard hoard of dirges,
dactyls, death songs. Our eyes
swallowed the guttural
black globes of oaths
on vellum's fleshed pages.
Runes streamed past us.
Shadows held forests
of meaning.
We tried to laugh
at that old language,
yet something held us.
We heard the roar
and blank of it:
the singer gone,
the great song
almost drowning.
Heart skewered,
we heard the swell
of silence. We stood
in the tide of it,
twenty-five twitching bodies
held by fate's branches.
As the ghost-fingered
librarian turned
pages on the battlefield
of ink, we saw the place
where a monk's hand
swept wide and sent
a glue pot guttering
right into us, here, in time.

The Wanderer *is an Anglo-Saxon elegy of exile contained in* The Exeter Book, *a manuscript of Old English poetry compiled in the late 10th century and held in the Exeter Cathedral Library.* The Exeter Book *comprises roughly one-sixth of all surviving Old English poetry.*

For Sandra, Who Drew a Tree

The things they asked meant nothing.
Here is a basket of seven apples,
take two away. How many left?
Enough to feed the mare.

They wanted her to trail
sentences: tail to toe, toe to tail.
To let worms letter their way
into words which squirmed
beneath her fingers.
She'd rather core an apple
with her father's knife.
There would be enough for raven.

She couldn't read these pale people,
their blank eyes seemed dead to fire.
She drank stories from rivers,
floated down streams, did not need
their writing sticks to remind her.
Verbs were water weeds slicked
to her skin, quiet thunder rumbling.
The teachers crossed her name off the list.

She understood from the look of them
that they were finished with her now.
So she let the pencil kiss the face
of the paper. One leap and a pine
rose to the wind. Mountains breathed
for a flock of redbirds to find them.
An eagle bristled, its eyes were sharp
as talons. A window cracked.
A tester turned away, felt sick
as the wildfire of this girl lit
and started catching.

Overheard: Ringing in the Changes

He wanted to chuck it all in.
To die then.
I helped him I think.
We ate beer, drank eggs
then we came here to ring.

The stream beyond the church
was in full spate.
Snowdrops sweet as
infants' fists nestled
in the ivy.

We struck the peal.
Half-muffled first,
but we kept on,
not knowing
where we might
range to ...

The changes ringing us
as we rang in the changes.

Why I Wear your Socks Today

I wear your socks today
so that I can see more deeply
into the old woman ahead of me
in the post office.

She is ashamed to be so slow.
She says, *Sorry, sorry* to the queue
as she shakes in her girlish jeans.
I repeat the words you taught me,

I too will die. I too will age.
I am not immune to suffering.
I wear your socks with their
bits of mud from the moor.

I have washed them twice,
still they breathe the wet and peat
reminding me that doubt like
water can be walked into and out of —

I wear your socks today
so that I can look into the face
of the mother of the child who
picking berries, blocks the path ...

Remembering the care of your
silence, I stop when this mother
breathes *Sorry, sorry.*
No need for sorry, I say.

There is no need.
This homeless man wends
his way to us, his three-legged
dog hopping along after.

We live in the sum
of sun and shadow,
in one another's seeing.
This is why I wear your socks today.

Understory

In these living gold-green
curtains of uncertainty,
the pendulous birch enacts
our cadences of living, falling
under the flame of sumac
where I listen to my husband
raking in October's end.
Tonight the quince waits
with its bright burn
of lanterns. The rust
of amber foliage eased
off by the western wind
becomes a bag-rustle of leaves.
Our long letting-go into winter
leads us to our harvest
of sparrow trill where songs
leak under the rag-ends of fire-
fall. Free from ambition, trees
live beauty from their core,
a carillon of rings, a silent music
we might yet learn to care for.

Life on Mars

Bereft of corn sow thistle,
I would not go
to a planet boiling
in red weather and so
lacking in the milky
dickle of green,
of fieldmouse and feather.

I would not trust a place
bereft of sow's bread,
meadows of Virgin Mary's
nipple, wood spurge,
wormwood, aconite's bane.

Where water is scarce,
dreams are hard.
Give me potatoes,
the gold flesh of suns,
our globe of stories,
barely begun.

Brent Geese Among Eelgrass

Pale-bellied, breaking flight,
they skid into paradise
into acres of eelgrass. Of light.
The ruffs of their feathers
are a busy biosphere of lice.
This might be the place
where Christ wheeled
with geese after he died.
That place where he lifted
the thieves who hung by his side
and fed them under the cover
of his wings, in an estuary of quiet.
And here is this boy-man,
skittish among graves,
taking cover behind a child
in a stroller. Fear rolls
back his eyes, the world
is a quick knife. He twitches.
Senses flayed raw,
he needs a needle to ice
his every other need.
To bury what's left of him,
alive. The trees have eyes.
He punches at his mobile.
'Where the fuck are you?'
And you?
             and you...
and you?
the collared doves reply.

Black Fire

He leaves the shed windows
open to welcome
their spittled nests,
to welcome the swift black
fire of our lives back
beneath this eave, a mud fist
nestled into this nothing-much
of time. We dip and soar
through our little space
of days. Wind calls
and we answer.
Black fire falling
between blows
of blossom, hail and ice.
We chance back
into sight. Sparks
light us into what we are:
spits of black fire.

Will Kemp Goes Dancing
In 1599 Will Kemp danced from London to Norwich; it is thought Shakespeare turned him down for the part of the clown in Hamlet.

Did I fail? Yes,
Yes, like Everyman,
yet what's the world
but wide? I took
a running-step off stage,
a headlong pitch.
I filched a hurdy-gurdy,
borrowed a cornet-
whistle. I had two feet.
A clown, I saw
death's laughing
maw would have me
soon enough. I learned
to love the rain.
If life rankled, I tried
a jig. A tune: *Rank
at the Rute,
The Lammas Vynde.*
Why not begin
again with new eyes?
I danced some hundred
miles. Each day my steps
became more lucid.
Was I a fool?
Yes. And yes!
Yet swans saw wonder
dawn on my face.
Exhaustion
bore me to the sea.
I leapt the river
of my breath
into all that is
and comes,
here and after.

Oversteps Books Ltd

The Oversteps list includes books by the following poets:

Jean Atkin, R V Bailey, Michael Bayley, Charles Bennett, Denise Bennett, Rebecca Bilkau, Patricia Bishop, Anne Born, Sue Boyle, Melanie Branton, David Broadbridge, Avril Bruton, Maggie Butt, Caroline Carver, Ian Royce Chamberlain, A C Clarke, Ross Cogan, James Cole, Robert Cole, Christopher Cook, Rose Cook, John Daniel, Miriam Darlington, Will Daunt, Sue Davies, Carol DeVaughn, Hilary Elfick, Jan Farquarson, Sally Festing, Rose Flint, Rebecca Gethin, Terry Gifford, Giles Goodland, Cora Greenhill, David Grubb, Charles Hadfield, Oz Hardwick, Jan Harris, Ken Head, Bill Headdon, Graham High, Doreen Hinchliffe, Jenny Hockey, Jenny Hope, Doris Hulme, Ann Kelley, Helen Kitson, Wendy Klein, Kathleen Kummer, Marianne Larsen, Patricia Leighton, Genista Lewes, Anne Lewis-Smith, Janet Loverseed, Mary Maher, Antony Mair, Alwyn Marriage, Marie Marshall, Fokkina McDonnell, Joan McGavin, Denise McSheehy, Andrew Nightingale, Christopher North, Jennie Osborne, Helen Overell, Mandy Pannett, Melanie Penycate, W H Petty, Glen Phillips, Sue Proffitt, Simon Richey, Lynn Roberts, Mary Robinson, Elisabeth Rowe, Ann Segrave, Richard Skinner, Alex Smith, Jane Spiro, Robert Stein, Anne Stewart, Angela Stoner, John Stuart, Paul Surman, Michael Swan, Diane Tang, Susan Taylor, Michael Thomas, John Torrance, Mark Totterdell, James Turner, Anthony Watts, Christine Whittemore and Simon Williams.

For details of all these books, information about Oversteps and up-to-date news, please look at our website and blog:

www.overstepsbooks.com
http://overstepsbooks.wordpress.com